HEALING YOUR
GRIEVING HEART
For Kids

Also by Alan Wolfelt:

A Child's View of Grief

*Creating Meaningful Funeral Ceremonies:
A Guide for Families*

*Healing a Child's Grieving Heart:
100 Practical Ideas for Families,
Friends and Caregivers*

*Healing a Teen's Grieving Heart:
100 Practical Ideas for Families,
Friends and Caregivers*

*Healing the Bereaved Child:
Grief Gardening,
Growth Through Grief and
Other Touchstones for Caregivers*

*Healing Your Grieving Heart for Teens:
100 Practical Ideas*

*The Journey Through Grief:
Reflections on Healing*

Understanding Grief: Helping Yourself Heal

*Companion Press is dedicated to the education
and support of both the bereaved and bereavement caregivers.*

*We believe that those who companion the bereaved
by walking with them as they journey in grief
have a wondrous opportunity: to help others embrace
and grow through grief—and to lead fuller,
more deeply-lived lives themselves
because of this important work.*

Companion
P R E S S

For a complete catalog
and ordering information, write or call:

Companion Press
The Center for Loss and Life Transition
3735 Broken Bow Road
Fort Collins, CO 80526
(970) 226-6050
www.centerforloss.com

HEALING YOUR GRIEVING HEART

For Kids

•

100 PRACTICAL IDEAS

•

ALAN D. WOLFELT, PH.D.

Companion
PRESS

Fort Collins, Colorado

An imprint of the Center for Loss and Life Transition

Library of Congress Catalog Card Number: 00-192969

Companion Press is an imprint of the
Center for Loss and Life Transition,
3735 Broken Bow Road, Fort Collins, Colorado 80526.

Companion Press books may be purchased in bulk for sales promotions, premiums or fundraisers. Please contact the publisher at the above address for more information.

Printed in Canada

10 09 08 07 06 05 04 03 02 01   5 4 3 2

ISBN: 1-879651-27-0

To the hundreds of grieving kids
I have had the privilege of
learning from over the past 25 years.
Thanks for teaching me.

A Note to Parents and Other Loving Grown-ups

This book is for children ages 6-12 who are grieving the death of someone they love. The basic message of the book is that children need to mourn — that is, to express their grief outside themselves — if they are to heal. They also need the compassionate support of adults like you.

Please read through this book before giving it to a child so you'll be able to help him or her with the 100 Ideas. You may need to read the book aloud to or along with 6-8 year-olds who are just starting to read independently.

Thank you for being a grown-up who helps children mourn well so they can go on to live well and love well.

Introduction

When I was a kid, one of my friends died. His name was Phil. We played on a baseball team together. Sometimes we went on long bike rides all over town. Then he got sick with a cancer called leukemia. He lived for awhile, but then he died.

I was very sad. I also had lots of questions. But nobody wanted to talk to me about the death! The grown-ups in my life thought they could protect me by *not* talking about it.

Inside, I felt lots of grief about the death. (Grief may be a word you haven't learned, but it just means the painful thoughts and feelings you have after someone you love dies.) The trouble was, I wasn't helped to let my grief out. I was confused and sad for a long, long time.

Now I'm a grown-up with kids of my own. I became a grief counselor. I've helped lots of grieving kids over the years. They've taught me many important lessons. The most important lesson grieving children have taught me is that they need to *mourn*.

Letting your grief out is called mourning. You need to mourn so you can start to feel better. If you don't mourn, your feelings will stay all bottled up inside like mine did.

I wrote this book to help you mourn. The 100 ideas give you ways to think about and feel your grief.

I'm sorry that someone you love has died. This is a very hard time for you. But I promise you this: If you let your grief out, and if you can find grown-ups who will help you with your mourning, you'll feel much better. And, over time, your life will be full of joy and happiness again.

You are special. You are loved. And you are so alive. I know you can do this. Mourn well and live well. Go for it.

Alan

1.

Learn that grief and mourning are different.

Grief (rhymes with leaf) is what you think and feel inside when someone you love dies. When you're in grief, you're *grieving* (rhymes with leaving).

Mourning (pronounced the same as morning) means letting those thoughts and feelings come out somehow.

You need to mourn so you can start to feel better. If you keep everything inside you'll only feel worse.

Write or draw your feelings about this:

2.

Take it easy on yourself.

The death of someone you love is probably the hardest thing you'll ever have to deal with. Go easy on yourself. This is going to take time.

Write or draw your feelings about this:

3.

UNDERSTAND THE SIX NEEDS OF MOURNING

Need 1.
Accept the death.

Someone you love is dead and can never come back. That's a tough thing to accept, but it's true.

Some days you may not want to think about the death. You may even want to pretend it never happened. That's OK, especially at first.

But soon you need to accept that this person really has died.

Write or draw your feelings about this:

4.

UNDERSTAND THE SIX NEEDS OF MOURNING

Need 2.
Let yourself feel sad.

Feeling sad is no fun. But you need to feel sad right now. Something really sad has happened in your life.

You don't need to feel sad every minute, though. You still need to laugh and play and be a kid. Let yourself feel happy, too.

Write or draw your feelings about this:

5.

UNDERSTAND THE SIX NEEDS OF MOURNING

Need 3.
Remember the person who died.

It's good to remember the person who died. Even though he or she can't be with you anymore, you'll always have your memories.

Talk about the person who died. Use his or her name. Look at pictures of him or her. Remember the fun times you had together.

Write or draw your feelings about this:

6.

UNDERSTAND THE SIX NEEDS OF MOURNING

Need 4.
Accept that your life is different now.

Your life is different now, isn't it? Think about how it's different.

Maybe your family has changed. Have you changed, too?

Your life will never be exactly the same again. But that doesn't mean it won't be happy again — just different.

Write or draw your feelings about this:

7.

UNDERSTAND THE SIX NEEDS OF MOURNING

Need 5.
Think about why this happened.

Why do people die? What happens to people after they die? You're probably asking yourself these kinds of questions.

It's good to think about the "whys" of life and death. Maybe you can talk about the "whys" with a parent or another adult you trust.

Write or draw your feelings about this:

8.

UNDERSTAND THE SIX NEEDS OF MOURNING

Need 6.
Let others help you, now and always.

Grief is so hard. You need people to love and help you through it.

Let others help you, especially grown-ups. It's OK to ask for help, too. Try talking to your family, your teacher or your neighbor.

Write or draw your feelings about this:

9.

Let yourself feel numb.

You know how your foot feels when you sit on it too long and it falls asleep? At first it feels completely numb, then it starts to tingle and hurt.

Your grief might feel like that too. At first you might feel nothing. That's OK. Soon you'll start to tingle and hurt. Let your feelings come little by little.

Write or draw your feelings about this:

10.

Let yourself feel whatever you feel.

Your grief isn't exactly like anyone else's. Your thoughts and feelings will be different.

It's OK to feel whatever you feel: sad, mad, maybe scared, sometimes even happy. No feelings are wrong or bad.

Write or draw your feelings about this:

11.

Talk to a grown-up you trust.

It's important to talk to grown-ups about your grief. Don't be afraid to ask questions — lots of questions.

Some grown-ups will be better than others at helping you with your grief. Find one or two grown-ups who make you feel safe and loved — and who will answer your questions openly and honestly. Talk to them.

Write or draw your feelings about this:

12.

Talk to a friend.

Your friends probably don't know what to say or do about your grief. Not many kids have had someone they love die.

But maybe you have one friend who's a really good listener. Talk to him or her about the death.

Write or draw your feelings about this:

13.

Talk about the person who died.

It's good to talk about the person who died. After all, this person was a big part of your life. And he or she will always be a part of your memories.

Talk about the death. Tell stories about him or her. Ask questions about the life of the person who died.

Write or draw your feelings about this:

14.

Cry.

Crying is *not* just for babies. Crying is for anyone —young or old — who feels sad. Crying helps your body let out its sadness.

Maybe you can find a grown-up who will hold you whenever you feel like crying.

Write or draw your feelings about this:

15.

Watch the sunrise.

The sun gets up really early, especially in the warmer months. But watching the sun's first rays peek out in the east can be an awesome experience. Find out what time the sun will rise tomorrow and set your alarm for 15 minutes earlier.

Write or draw your feelings about this:

16.

Get lots of sleep.

Grief can really tire you out. Your body might need extra sleep right now.

Go to bed early if you're feeling tired. Take a nap after school if you need to.

Write or draw your feelings about this:

17.

Eat foods that are good for you.

Grief is hard work. Your body will feel better if you give it good fuel right now.

Try to eat food from all the different food groups every day.

Write or draw your feelings about this:

18.

Drink lots of water.

One funny thing about grief is that it can make you feel like not eating or drinking very much. But your body actually needs *more* food and water right now.

Get in the habit of drinking from water fountains whenever you see one. Drink a glass of water after school every day.

Write or draw your feelings about this:

19.

Play outside.

Lots of times, just being outside will make you feel better. Especially if it's a really nice day.

Go outside and kick a ball around. Roll down a hill. Climb a tree.

Write or draw your feelings about this:

20.

Find a "grief hide-out."

Maybe you can find a private spot to go when you want to be alone with your grief. It could be a fort in your backyard or a quiet place somewhere in your house.

When you're in your grief hide-out, you can cry, write, draw or just sit and think.

Write or draw your feelings about this:

21.

Don't be alone
too much.

If you want to be alone with your grief
sometimes, that's OK. Go to your room
or your grief hide-out and cry or write in
your journal or just think.

But don't cut off other people when they
want to spend time with you or talk to
you. It's important for you to let others
help you right now.

Write or draw your feelings about this:

22.

Let yourself feel happy.

Just because something sad has happened in your life doesn't mean you should always feel sad. Do something every day that makes you feel happy. Smile, laugh and play. Be a kid.

Write or draw your feelings about this:

23.

Play with a pet.

Pets can be great friends. They're always there when you need them. They love you no matter what.

If you have a pet, spend some special time with it today. If you don't have a pet, visit a pet shop or play with a neighbor's pet. (Ask permission first.)

Write or draw your feelings about this:

24.

Go to church or your family's place of worship.

Does your family belong to a church or other place of worship? If so, going once a week or so will probably help you with your grief. Now might also be a good time to join a church youth group or church choir.

If your family doesn't attend a church or other place of worship, maybe you could ask them to consider taking you sometime.

Write or draw your feelings about this:

25.

Keep a journal.

Writing down your grief thoughts and feelings is a great way to mourn. You can write as much or as little as you want. Write whenever you feel like it. When you're writing in your journal, you can also pretend you're writing to the person who died.

Write or draw your feelings about this:

26.

Draw out
your feelings.

Making art is another great way to mourn.
You can draw, paint, mold clay, paste
together a collage, assemble a sculpture —
whatever you feel like. Try to put your
grief feelings into your artwork.

Write or draw your feelings about this:

27.

Dance.

When you dance, you let your thoughts go and just let your body move to the music. Dancing is good to try when you need a break from your grief. Dancing can also be a way for your body to express your grief.

Write or draw your feelings about this:

28.

Play sports.

Sports do all kinds of good things for you. They keep your body in shape. They teach you how to win and how to lose. They get you involved with other kids. They make you feel better about yourself. Join a sports team this season.

Write or draw your feelings about this:

29.

Play games.

When you feel like doing something fun, play a game. Get a friend to play Monopoly or checkers with you. Play hopscotch or HORSE. Ask a grown-up to teach you how to play chess.

Write or draw your feelings about this:

30.

Write a letter to the person who died.

Maybe you wish you could say something to the person who died. Write it down in a letter. You can read the letter to a grown-up or bring the letter to the cemetery and read it to the person who died. Or you can just tuck it away and read it later to yourself.

Write or draw your feelings about this:

31.

Make a memory book.

A memory book is a photo album or scrapbook filled with memories of the person who died. You can include photos, drawings and souvenirs. When you're done you'll have a book you can look through whenever you're missing the person who died.

Write or draw your feelings about this:

32.

Pack a memory box.

A memory box is even easier than a memory book; you just put things that remind you of the person who died in a box. The box can be as big or as small as you want. Fill it with pictures, souvenirs, things that belonged to the person who died, and maybe even videotapes.

Write or draw your feelings about this:

33.

Hold onto something that belonged to the person who died.

When you were smaller you might have had a special blanket or teddy bear that made you feel safe. Maybe now you can hold onto something special that belonged to the person who died, like a favorite shirt or a toy. Choose something that reminds you of happy times together.

Write or draw your feelings about this:

34.

Plant a garden.

Do you have a place where you can plant flowers or vegetables? Digging in the dirt is lots of fun. And it's amazing to watch a tiny seed grow into a tall sunflower or a super long zucchini.

Write or draw your feelings about this:

35.

Tell your friends and family that you love them.

Maybe this death has made you realize how special certain people are to you. Tell them you love them. Do something nice for them for no special reason.

Write or draw your feelings about this:

36.

Hug.

It's amazing how much better you can feel just by hugging someone you love. Hug your family today. Hug a friend.

Write or draw your feelings about this:

37.

Hold hands.

Do you ever hold hands with people in your family or with a friend? It feels good to be connected to someone else.

Write or draw your feelings about this:

38.

Clean your room.

Grief can make your life feel pretty mixed up. One way to feel more in control is to clean your room. You might be surprised how much better you feel when you have a clean, orderly room to come home to everyday.

Start with one shelf or drawer and see if it works for you.

Write or draw your feelings about this:

39.

Pray.

Have you been taught to pray? If so, now's a good time to practice. Try saying a prayer at bedtime every night. If you don't know how to pray, just close your eyes and silently ask God for help. Tell God about the person who died. Explain your thoughts and feelings.

Write or draw your feelings about this:

40.

Be silly.

Sometimes it's good to be silly when your grief is making you feel too serious. Go totally crazy. Wear underwear on your head. Dance like a chicken.

Write or draw your feelings about this:

41.

Laugh.

What makes you laugh? Cartoons? Being tickled? A good joke?

Laugh like crazy today. Laughing doesn't mean you don't love the person who died.

Write or draw your feelings about this:

42.

Put up pictures of the person who died.

It's good to look at pictures of the person who died and remember all the special things about him or her. Hang some up in your bedroom. Keep one in your pocket if you want. Put one in your backpack.

Write or draw your feelings about this:

43.

If you're having trouble with your schoolwork, talk to a grown-up about it.

This might be a rough time for you at school. It can be hard to work on reading and math when all you can think about is the person who died.

If your grief is making school hard for you right now, talk to a grown-up about it. Talk to a parent, an adult friend or your teacher. Someone can help you make a plan for getting back on track at school.

Write or draw your feelings about this:

44.

Join a grief support group for kids.

Talking to other grieving kids can feel really good. It helps you know that you're not the only one. You'll also make friends and get some good ideas for living with your grief.

Many towns have support groups for grieving kids. Your school or local hospice might have one.

With an adult's permission, you could also visit a web support group for kids called kids-to-kids. You'll find it at www.kidsaid.com.

Write or draw your feelings about this:

45.

Talk to other kids who are grieving.

You don't have to join a support group to talk to other grieving kids. Maybe you know someone at school who has had a death in the family. Or maybe you have cousins or brothers and sisters or friends who are grieving the same death you are. Ask them how they're doing. Ask them if they think about the person who died.

Write or draw your feelings about this:

46.

Talk to a counselor.

Talking about your grief to grown-ups who care about you is always a good idea. Counselors who've helped other grieving kids can really be great to talk to.

If your parent or teacher suggests you see a counselor, give it a try. You'll be helping yourself feel better.

Write or draw your feelings about this:

47.

Do something you're good at.

Everybody's good at something. What are you good at? Running? Penmanship? Making peanut butter and jelly sandwiches?

Do something you're good at today. It'll make you feel good about yourself — and you'll probably have fun!

Write or draw your feelings about this:

48.

Do something you're not so good at.

Doing something you're not so good at
helps you learn to think with an open
mind. Don't get frustrated, just
concentrate on learning and having fun.
Besides, if you practice, you'll get better.

Write or draw your feelings about this:

49.

Eat something weird.

Life is for trying new things. Today, eat something you've never tried before. Don't expect it to be gross. Instead, convince yourself you're going to like it —and maybe you will!

Write or draw your feelings about this:

50.

Don't be scared by "griefbursts."

Sometimes, out of nowhere, you will feel a wave of sadness you didn't expect. These "griefbursts" can be scary.

When you have a griefburst, find someone you can talk to about it. Or just snuggle up with a grown-up who loves you and sit quietly until it passes.

Write or draw your feelings about this:

51.

Look for your grief on special days.

Your grief will probably pop up on certain days, like your birthday or the birthday of the person who died, Christmas, Hanukkah, the anniversary of the death. These days can be really hard. Ask a grown-up who cares about you to spend some time with you on these days.

Write or draw your feelings about this:

52.

Do something that the person who died would have liked.

The person who died probably really liked doing this or that. Maybe he liked to play cards. Or maybe she loved chocolate cake. Think of something he or she really liked and do it today. Ask a grown-up for permission if it's something you can't do yourself.

Write or draw your feelings about this:

53.

Listen to music.

Music can help you express your feelings. Try listening to classical music when you want to think about the death. Put on some rock & roll when you're feeling happy.

What kind of music did the person who died like? Maybe you can listen to that music when you want to remember him or her.

Write or draw your feelings about this:

54.

Visit the cemetery.

It's good to visit the grave of the person who died. It can help you feel close to him or her. It's also a quiet place to think and feel your grief. If the person wasn't buried, maybe you can visit the spot where the ashes were scattered, or a special place that reminds you of him or her.

Ask a grown-up to come with you.

Write or draw your feelings about this:

55.

Don't think you have to be strong.

Don't try to be "strong" in grief. Let others know what you're really thinking and feeling. Remember, mourning means letting your grief out. Don't hide what's going on inside.

Actually, if you mourn you're being strong because mourning is hard work.

Write or draw your feelings about this:

56.

If you're feeling extra sad, talk to someone.

Sometimes you might feel really, really sad. Or maybe you're feeling really, really sad all the time.

Talk to a grown-up you trust about your sad feelings. Maybe you need some extra help with your feelings right now.

Write or draw your feelings about this:

57.

Never do something that might hurt you or others.

Hurting yourself or someone else is never OK. Your life is hard right now, but it will get better. Lots better. People love you. You're a special kid.

If you're having scary thoughts about hurting yourself or someone else, talk to a grown-up you trust right away.

Write or draw your feelings about this:

58.

Write a poem.

Poetry is a good way to shape thoughts and feelings. Write a poem about the person who died. It doesn't have to rhyme or have any certain form. Try starting out with this line: "Before you died …" Or this one: "When I think of you, I remember … "

Write or draw your feelings about this:

59.

List the things that are still good about your life.

Sometimes when we're grieving we forget about the good things in our lives. But there are tons of them! Make a list right now. Be as specific as you can.

Write or draw your feelings about this:

60.

Know that
people love you.

Lots of people care about you. You're a
special kid and many people love you.

You may want to make a list of these
people or draw a picture of each one.

Write or draw your feelings about this:

61.

Appreciate yourself.

You are a pretty awesome kid — do you know that? Think about all the reasons that you're special. Mainly you're special because you were born into this unique family and community at this unique time. And your family and community just wouldn't be the same without you!

Write or draw your feelings about this:

62.

Play out your grief.

Playing is what kids are supposed to do —
even grieving kids. Have fun playing
every day. If you feel like letting out
some of your grief feelings in your play,
that's good. For example, you could take
out mad feelings by kicking a ball or
express tender feelings by playing with
your stuffed animals.

Write or draw your feelings about this:

63.

Join a club.

Getting involved in a club or new activity might really help you right now. Consider Girl/Boy Scouts, 4-H, a local soccer team, karate—anything that sounds fun and involves other kids!

Write or draw your feelings about this:

64.

Don't let anyone take away your grief.

You know what? Your grief is yours. You have the right to think and feel all your unique thoughts and feelings. If someone says you shouldn't feel the way you do, don't believe it. Instead, choose to talk to someone who will accept your grief and help you through it.

Write or draw your feelings about this:

65.

If you are a boy, think about this:

Sometimes grieving boys are told they have to "be strong" or "be a man." If one of your parents has died, you might really feel pressured to grow up too quickly. But you're still a kid! You're *not* a "man" yet. You still need lots of help with your grief and all the other regular kid things going on in your life.

Write or draw your feelings about this:

66.

If you are a girl, think about this:

Sometimes grieving girls are expected to cry and be sad all the time. If you're not feeling especially sad today, that's OK. It's OK to play and have fun when you want to.

Sometimes grieving girls are expected to take over chores at home, especially if a parent dies. It's good to help out around the house but remember that you're just a kid. You shouldn't have to take care of brothers and sisters too much or cook and clean too much.

Write or draw your feelings about this:

67.

Make a wish.

Close your eyes and wish for something you really want. The person who died can't come back, but maybe you have another wish that's really possible! Wish the wish then work to make it happen.

Write or draw your feelings about this:

68.

Do something nice for someone else.

Doing something nice for someone else helps both of you feel good. Do something nice for someone else today for no special reason. Make a drawing and give it to your parents, play a game your brother or sister or friend wants to play, rake your neighbor's leaves.

Write or draw your feelings about this:

69.

Help your family mourn.

Sometimes families have to learn how to mourn well. Encourage your family to talk about the death. Share memories of the person who died whenever you feel like it. Ask your family to visit the cemetery or scattering place with you.

Write or draw your feelings about this:

70.

Make music.

Even if you don't know how to play a musical instrument, you can make music. Blow on a harmonica or plastic flute. Set up some pots and pans on your floor and play the drums. Put on a CD and pretend you're playing the guitar or conducting the orchestra.

Write or draw your feelings about this:

71.

Have a sleep-over.

First get permission, then invite a friend or two to sleep over this weekend. Plan to stay up late and have lots of fun. If you end up talking late at night with your friend, you might want to talk about your grief so he or she knows how you've been feeling.

Write or draw your feelings about this:

72.

Write a story.

Once upon a time there was a kid who was feeling really sad because ... Make up the rest of this story and write it down. Later on, read your story to a grown-up who loves you.

Be sure to save your story and read it again a few months from now. See if your story feels different then.

Write or draw your feelings about this:

73.

Hang out with people who make you feel good and safe.

Some people are good at helping grieving kids. Some are not. When you're feeling your grief, spend time with people who make you feel good and safe.

Write or draw your feelings about this:

74.

Don't let other kids get to you.

Lots of kids won't know how to talk to you about your grief. Some kids might even tease you or say mean things.

Mostly kids act this way because they're scared. They're scared that someone they love could die, too. Try not to let them get to you. Find a friend who understands or won't hurt your feelings.

Write or draw your feelings about this:

75.

Learn something new.

What have you always wanted to learn how to do? Juggle? Do a cartwheel? Whistle through your fingers? Skateboard? Whatever it is, practice doing it today. If you know someone who's good at it, ask them to teach you.

Write or draw your feelings about this:

76.

If you're feeling mad, do this:

You might feel mad that someone you love has died. It's OK to feel this way. But it's not OK to hurt anyone or anything when you feel mad. Instead, punch a pillow. Or close your bedroom door and scream. Or draw an angry drawing.

Write or draw your feelings about this:

77.

If you're feeling afraid, do this:

Sometimes death makes us feel afraid — even grown-ups. The best thing to do when you're feeling afraid is to talk to someone about your fears. Find a grown-up who loves you, give him or her a hug and say, "I'm scared because ..."

Write or draw your feelings about this:

78.

If you're feeling guilty, do this:

Sometimes grieving kids feel like the death was their fault. Maybe there was a time when you wished the person would die. Or maybe you feel like you caused the death somehow. You didn't!

It's normal to feel these feelings, but you didn't do anything wrong! Talk to a grown-up about your guilty feelings soon.

Write or draw your feelings about this:

79.

If you're feeling relieved, do this:

You might be feeling relieved about this death. Maybe the person who died was very sick and death has brought him or her peace. Or maybe you have mixed feelings about the person who died. Maybe you loved the person but didn't like things he or she did.

It's OK to feel relieved when someone dies. You can feel lots of different feelings all at once if you want.

Write or draw your feelings about this:

80.

If you've been behaving badly, do this:

Sometimes grief makes us misbehave. Sometimes our feelings are mixed up or get to be too much and we say or do bad things.

If you've been behaving badly, talk to a grown-up about it. Maybe he or she can help you figure out a better way to handle your feelings.

Write or draw your feelings about this:

81.

Be a big baby.

When you're grieving, it's OK to do things that seem babyish. It's natural to want to cry, be held, snuggle with grown-ups, hug a stuffed animal. For now it's OK to do whatever makes you feel safe and gives you comfort.

Write or draw your feelings about this:

82.

Read a book.

Have you read a good book lately?
Sometimes story books are a good way to
relax and hide away from your life for an
hour or two.

Write or draw your feelings about this:

83.

Don't watch too much TV.

It's tempting to watch TV a lot, especially when we're feeling bad. TV shows take our minds off our lives.

But watching too much TV won't make your grief go away — it will only put it off until later. And later it will be even harder.

Write or draw your feelings about this:

84.

Talk to your teacher.

Teachers can sometimes be great grief
helpers — if you let them. Talk to your
teacher about the death. Let him or her
know if you're having a hard time with
your schoolwork because of your grief.
Ask your teacher to help if other kids
are teasing you or being mean about
the death.

Write or draw your feelings about this:

85.

Talk to your grandparents.

Do you have grandparents or family friends who are older? They've been around a long time. They've probably had many people they love die over the years. Talk to them about your grief. Ask them to tell you stories from their past.

If you don't live near your grandparents, write them a letter or call them on the phone. If they're online, send them an e-mail!

Write or draw your feelings about this:

86.

Talk to your brother or sister.

If you have brothers or sisters, they've probably been hurt by this death, too. It's good to talk to them about your feelings and ask them about theirs. Spend time hanging out or playing together. Be gentle and understanding.

If you're fighting a lot with your brothers and sisters right now, it could be because of the death. Grief can make people upset and grouchy.

Write or draw your feelings about this:

87.

Think of all the people you love.

Someone you love has died. But many people you love are still here with you — and will be here to laugh with and take care of you and love you for many, many years to come. Their love will help carry you through this hard time.

Write or draw your feelings about this:

88.

Dress up like someone else.

Right now you might wish that you could be someone else, maybe someone whose life seems perfect.

Pretend you're someone else. Play dress up if you want. Imagine what that person's life is like and enjoy it for an hour or two.

Write or draw your feelings about this:

89.

Know that your grief is special.

Your grief is yours. No one else will think exactly what you think or feel exactly what you feel. Your grief is special — just like you.

Write or draw your feelings about this:

90.

If your body hurts, tell a grown-up.

Does your body hurt somewhere? Are you afraid that you might be sick or dying, too? If your answer is yes to either of these questions, talk to a grown-up you trust. Your body is probably just fine, but a quick check-up at the doctor's office might help you not worry.

Write or draw your feelings about this:

91.

Sing.

You probably know lots of songs, but do you sing them? Try it today. Sing in the shower. Or crank up a CD and sing in your bedroom. Your singing voice doesn't have to be great; it'll feel good just to let yourself be heard.

Write or draw your feelings about this:

92.

Be you.

This death has changed your life but you're still you. However you were before the death — shy, outgoing, clownish, serious — you'll probably handle your grief in the same way. Be yourself.

Write or draw your feelings about this:

93.

Start a business.

Maybe you don't know what to do with yourself when you're not at school. Start a business! If you're old enough, you can babysit or mow lawns. If you're younger, you can do extra chores around the house. Or maybe you have a great idea for a new invention. Give it a try!

Write or draw your feelings about this:

94.

Give a gift.

You've probably heard this saying before: It's better to give than to receive. Giving makes you feel really good inside. Give a gift to someone you love today for no special reason. The gift doesn't have to be something you buy. You could paint a picture or write a poem or collect some cool rocks.

Write or draw your feelings about this:

95.

Be a friend to someone else who's grieving this death.

Who else is grieving this death? Probably lots of people. Pick one person and be especially nice to that person today. Maybe the two of you can even talk about your feelings about the death.

Write or draw your feelings about this:

96.

Smile.

When you're feeling sad and are ready to feel better, try smiling. Just lifting up the corners of your mouth may help you think happy thoughts. Smile at other kids at school — they'll probably smile back.

Write or draw your feelings about this:

97.

Look at the sky.

Lie on your back and look at the sky. During the day, the sun and clouds can make you feel peaceful. At night, the stars and planets can make you feel like part of something really important. Do you believe in heaven? Look at the sky and imagine what it's like.

Write or draw your feelings about this:

98.

Understand that your grief will last a long time.

Your grief will last a long time. You'll never stop missing the person who died. But as time passes you won't feel so sad about the death. You'll probably think about the person less often. That's OK; you can still love someone in your memories.

Memories made in love — no one can ever take them away from you!

Write or draw your feelings about this:

99.

Believe that you will, one day, learn to "reconcile" your grief.

You'll never completely "get over" this death, but you'll learn to accept it as part of your life. You'll learn to live with it. This is what "reconcile" means. You'll also learn that your life can be full of meaning and happiness again.

Write or draw your feelings about this:

100.

Dream about your future.

Your life is full of so much possibility. You can do anything you want to do. You can be anything you want to be. Your future is yours to create.

Write or draw your feelings about this:

A Final Word

I hope you've tried some of the ideas in this book. Mostly I hope that you've learned how important it is for you to mourn — to let your grief out.

If you mourn and if you have people around you — especially grown-ups — to help you mourn, you will get through this. You'll never completely get over the death or missing the person who died, but you will be happy again. Your life will be wonderful and full of love.

Sometimes I say that flowers are a lot like grieving kids. Like a flower after a hard spring rain, you're probably feeling fragile and battered right now. The flower needs sun and the gentle tending of the gardener. You need love and the help of grown-ups.

If you get what you need, you'll heal from this death. You'll unfurl your beautiful petals and soak up the sunshine of life.

My Grief Rights

1. **I have the right to have my own unique feelings about the death.**
   I might feel mad, sad or lonely. I might feel scared or relieved. I might feel numb or sometimes not anything at all. No one will feel exactly like I do.

2. **I have the right to talk about my grief whenever I feel like talking.**
   When I need to talk, I will find someone who will listen to me and love me. When I don't want to talk, that's OK, too.

3. **I have the right to show my feelings of grief in my own way.**
   When they are hurting, some kids like to play so they'll feel better for awhile. I can play or laugh, too. I might also get mad and misbehave. This does not mean I am bad; it just means I have scary feelings that I need help with.

4. **I have the right to need other people to help me with my grief,**
   especially grown-ups who care about me. Mostly I need them to pay attention to what I am feeling and saying and to love me no matter what.

5. **I have the right to get upset about normal, everyday problems.**
   I might feel grumpy and have trouble getting along with others sometimes.

6. **I have the right to have "griefbursts."**
Griefbursts are sudden, unexpected feelings of
sadness that just hit me sometimes — even long
after the death. These feelings can be very strong and
even scary. When this happens, I might feel afraid
to be alone.

7. **I have the right to use my beliefs about God to
help me with my grief.**
Praying might make me feel better and somehow
closer to the person who died.

8. **I have the right to try to figure out *why* the
person I loved died.**
But it's OK if I don't find an answer. "Why"
questions about life and death are the hardest
questions in the world.

9. **I have the right to think and talk about my
memories of the person who died.**
Sometimes those memories will be happy and
sometimes they might be sad. Either way, memories
help me keep alive my love for the person who died.

10. **I have the right to move toward and feel my grief
and, over time, to heal.**
I'll go on to live a happy life, but the life and death
of the person who died will always be a part of me.
I'll always miss the person who died.

*"My Grief Rights" is available as a neat kids' poster. See the
last page of this book for details.*

Glossary of Terms

Bereaved   When someone is in mourning we
sometimes say they are "bereaved."
Actually, the word bereaved means to
be "torn apart." Kind of fitting, huh?

Deceased   Another word for the person who
died. (I don't like the term deceased
because it sounds so impersonal.)

Grief   All the thoughts and feelings you
have on the inside when someone
you love dies.

Griefburst   Sudden and strong feelings of
sadness, sometimes long after the
death. Griefbursts are normal but can
be really hard. If a griefburst bursts
in on you, let a grown-up know how
you're feeling.

Mourning   Letting your grief out by talking about
it, writing about it, playing it out,
crying, doing activities that help you
think about the person who died, etc.

Reconcile   This is a word I use to describe what happens when people begin to heal in grief. To reconcile your grief means to learn to live with your grief and to go on with a happy, full life. Reconciliation happens when you mourn well and are supported by people who love you.

Support group   A group of people who get together to talk about similar experiences. Grief support groups for kids bring together children who have experienced the death of someone loved. Support groups can be a great way to help you mourn.

Send us your ideas for Healing Your Grieving Heart!

I'd love to hear your ideas for healing grief. I may use them in other books someday. Please jot down your idea below and mail or e-mail it to:

Dr. Alan Wolfelt,
The Center for Loss and Life Transition
3735 Broken Bow Rd.
Fort Collins, CO 80526
wolfelt@centerforloss.com

I can't wait to hear from you!

My idea:

_____

_____

_____

_____

My name, age and mailing/e-mail address:

_____

_____

_____

Also By
Dr. Alan Wolfelt

HEALING A CHILD'S GRIEVING HEART
100 PRACTICAL IDEAS FOR FAMILIES, FRIENDS & CAREGIVERS

An idea book for grown-ups who want practical, day-to-day "how-tos" for helping the grieving children they love. Some of the ideas teach about children's unique mourning styles and needs. Others suggest simple activities and tips for spending time together. A compassionate, easy-to-read resource for parents, aunts and uncles, grandparents, teachers, volunteers and a great refresher for professional caregivers.

ISBN 1-879651-28-9
128 pages • Softcover • $11.95
(plus additional shipping and handling)

Companion
P R E S S

All Dr. Wolfelt's publications can be ordered by mail from:

Companion Press
3735 Broken Bow Road • Fort Collins, CO 80526
(970) 226-6050 • Fax 1-800-922-6051
www.centerforloss.com

OTHER TITLES IN THE POPULAR 100 IDEAS SERIES:

HEALING YOUR GRIEVING HEART: 100 PRACTICAL IDEAS

Someone you love has died. What do you do with all these difficult thoughts and feelings you're having? This book offers 100 practical, compassionate ideas for healing.

ISBN 1-879651-25-4
128 pages • Softcover • $11.95
(plus additional shipping and handling)

HEALING A FRIEND'S GRIEVING HEART: 100 PRACTICAL IDEAS FOR HELPING SOMEONE YOU LOVE THROUGH LOSS

What do you say? What shouldn't you say? What can you do? This practical guide suggests 100 ideas for being a good friend to someone in grief.

ISBN 1-879651-26-2
128 pages • Softcover • $11.95
(plus additional shipping and handling)

HEALING YOUR GRIEVING HEART FOR TEENS: 100 PRACTICAL IDEAS

Grief is especially difficult during the teen years. This book explains why this is so and offers straightforward, practical advice for healing.

ISBN 1-879651-23-8
128 pages • Softcover • $11.95
(plus additional shipping and handling)

HEALING A TEEN'S GRIEVING HEART: 100 PRACTICAL IDEAS FOR FAMILIES, FRIENDS & CAREGIVERS

If you want to help a grieving teen but aren't sure how, this book is for you. It explains the teen's unique mourning needs, offers real-world advice and suggests realistic activities.

ISBN 1-879651-24-6
128 pages • Softcover • $11.95
(plus additional shipping and handling)

HEALING THE BEREAVED CHILD:
GRIEF GARDENING, GROWTH THROUGH GRIEF AND OTHER TOUCHSTONES FOR CAREGIVERS

One spring morning a gardener noticed an unfamiliar seedling poking through the ground near the rocky, untended edge of his garden... So begins the parable that sets the tone for this inspiring heartfelt book for caregivers to bereaved children. By comparing grief counseling to gardening, Dr. Wolfelt frees caregivers of the traditional medical model of bereavement care, suggesting instead that caregivers instead embrace a more holistic view of the normal, natural and necessary process that is grief.

Chapter after chapter of practical caregiving guidelines, including: how a grieving child thinks, feels and mourns; what makes each child's grief unique; the six needs of mourning; foundations of counseling bereaved children; counseling techniques; support groups for bereaved kids; helping grieving children at school; helping the grieving adolescent; and more!

ISBN 1-879651-10-6
8 1/2" x 11" format • 344 pages • Softcover • $39.95
(plus additional shipping and handling)

Companion
PRESS

All Dr. Wolfelt's publications can be ordered by mail from:

Companion Press
3735 Broken Bow Road • Fort Collins, CO 80526
(970) 226-6050 • Fax 1-800-922-6051
www.centerforloss.com

HOW I FEEL
A COLORING BOOK FOR GRIEVING CHILDREN

Dr. Wolfelt's coloring book for kids ages 3-8 explores many of the feelings grieving children often experience. The expressive, easy-to-color drawings clearly depict disbelief, fear, anger, loneliness, happiness, sadness and other normal grief feelings. The simple text accompanying the drawings "Someone I love has died;" "Ever since this person died, I have felt new and scary feelings. Grown-ups call these feelings grief." gives children words to describe their new, sometimes scary feelings.

ISBN 1-879651-17-3
24 pages • $2.00
(plus $2 S&H for a single copy)

Bulk order discount • 25 copies • $30.00
(plus regular S&H)

Companion
P R E S S

All Dr. Wolfelt's publications can be ordered by mail from:

Companion Press
3735 Broken Bow Road • Fort Collins, CO 80526
(970) 226-6050 • Fax 1-800-922-6051
www.centerforloss.com

A CHILD'S VIEW OF GRIEF
Book and Videotape

In this informative, easy-to-read booklet, Dr. Wolfelt explains how children and adolescents grieve after someone loved dies and offers helping guidelines for caregiving adults. An excellent, concise resource for parents of grieving kids. The companion videotape, written by and featuring Dr. Wolfelt as well as actual bereaved children and their families, explores several key principles of helping children cope with grief.

Booklet • ISBN 1-879651-00-9
45 pages • Softcover • $5.95
(plus additional shipping and handling)

Videotape • 20 minutes • $64.95
(plus additional shipping and handling)

Companion
P R E S S

All Dr. Wolfelt's publications can be ordered by mail from:

Companion Press
3735 Broken Bow Road • Fort Collins, CO 80526
(970) 226-6050 • Fax 1-800-922-6051
www.centerforloss.com

A TEEN'S VIEW OF GRIEF:
AN EDUCATIONAL VIDEOTAPE FOR BEREAVEMENT CAREGIVERS

This fresh video on teen grief, written by and featuring Dr. Wolfelt, explodes with in-depth information in its beautifully produced forty minutes: adolescent tasks complicated by grief; nature of the deaths encountered by teens; the grieving teen's support systems and mourning needs; signs a teen may need extra help and more.

"Alan Wolfelt does it again. This groundbreaking video is a comprehensive, succinct, compassionate view of the special kind of mourning that occurs at this important transitional time. The heart and soul of the bereaved teen is carefully uncovered by Wolfelt and couched in his own inimitable understanding."

SUSIE KUSZMAR,
HOSPICE OF FRESNO AT SAINT AGNES

Videotape • 40 minutes • $99.95
(plus additional shipping and handling)

Companion
PRESS

All Dr. Wolfelt's publications can be ordered by mail from:

Companion Press
3735 Broken Bow Road • Fort Collins, CO 80526
(970) 226-6050 • Fax 1-800-922-6051
www.centerforloss.com

SARAH'S JOURNEY

Eight-year-old Sarah Johnson had always been her "daddy's little girl" until the tragic day her father was killed in a car accident. Based on the belief that each child has the need to mourn in his or her own way, this book describes Sarah's grief experiences and offers compassionate, practical advice for adults on topics such as regressive behaviors, explosive emotions, children and funerals, the grieving child at school and more.

ISBN 1-879651-03-3
121 pages • Softcover • $9.95
(plus additional shipping and handling)

Companion
P R E S S

All Dr. Wolfelt's publications can be ordered by mail from:

Companion Press
3735 Broken Bow Road • Fort Collins, CO 80526
(970) 226-6050 • Fax 1-800-922-6051
www.centerforloss.com

MY GRIEF RIGHTS
A Poster for Grieving Kids

This colorful, oversized poster helps grieving kids understand their feelings and empowers them to mourn in healthy ways. A compassionate gift for any bereaved child old enough to read. The contemporary design and straightforward-but-not-condescending text also make it appropriate for grieving teenagers. Sized to fit a standard, ready-made frame.

Poster (24" x 36") • $10.00
(plus additional shipping and handling)

Companion
P R E S S

All Dr. Wolfelt's publications can be ordered by mail from:

Companion Press
3735 Broken Bow Road • Fort Collins, CO 80526
(970) 226-6050 • Fax 1-800-922-6051
www.centerforloss.com